TONI ONLEY A SILENT THUNDER

Blanchard Peak over Pitt Lake, B.C. January 30 1981   Onley

ROGER H. BOULET

TONI ONLEY

CEREBRUS
PRENTICE HALL

A SILENT THUNDER

Canadian Cataloguing in Publication Data

Boulet, Roger, 1944 –
Toni Onley: a silent thunder

ISBN 0-920016-11-1 (Cerebrus Publishing)
ISBN 0-13-924803-X (Prentice Hall)

1. Onley, Toni, 1928 – I. Onley, Toni, 1928 –
II. Title: Toni Onley: a silent thunder.

ND249. 054A4 1981   759. II   C81-094689-0

Concept: Bernard Loates

Design and Production: John Orr

Typesetting: Words Over North America Inc.

In writing and researching this essay on Toni Onley's watercolor paintings, I received great cooperation from the artist whose patience and understanding were tremendous. I wish to thank him for making my task both easy and enjoyable from the very beginning. Many thanks also to Yukiko Onley who made long interviews all the more pleasant with coffee, tea and all sorts of edible delicacies, and who answered my many questions about Japanese brushes and aesthetics. I would also like to express belated thanks to Mrs. Joan Stanley-Baker who was the first to make me aware of the Chinese and Japanese ways of painting when we worked together from 1975 to 1980 at the Art Gallery of Greater Victoria.

Roger H. Boulet Vancouver, April 14, 1981

FOREWORD

TO MY WIFE   YUKIKO

                              SHE WAS MY FIRST MEETING
                              WITH THE ORIENT

My earliest memory of painting in watercolor is from grade one at the Catholic school I attended on the Isle of Man. The beginning years were taught by nuns. Once my teacher had set us the task of painting a daffodil. I thought I had done very well because even then I knew I was an artist, but my teacher pointed out with her cane that a daffodil had six petals, not seven as I had painted. I remember being beaten with her cane to drive home the lesson: my teacher later became known as Our Lady of Perpetual Suffering. The memory of her, her litany of punishments and the seven petalled daffodil have become branded in my mind forever.

The minutes of school chained to a desk passed like hours, just waiting for the long summer holidays which I would always spend with my paternal grandparents in the little town of Ramsey in the north of the Island.

My grandmother, who was an Irish lady from Queenstown (now Cork) county Cork always claimed my talent for painting came from her, because as a girl she had designed Irish lace. I was 10 years old and remember going on long walks with her on summer afternoons through glens and mountains, along coastal trails, she with her book of verse and me with my little box of watercolors. We would rest on the brow of a hill, I would paint and she would read to me, Wordsworth or Keats.

PHOTO: IMAO MATSUO

Toni Onley, 1981.

I was about fourteen before I received any formal art training. I enrolled in the Douglas School of Art in my hometown, where I was taught perspective, illuminated addressing, uncial script and the studious copying of the Book of Kells. We were taught life drawing and etching. Apart from illuminated addressing, which has influenced my handwriting ever since, I cannot remember learning anything of lasting value. However it was at this time that I fell under the influence of John Hobbs Nicholson, the lettering teacher. He was a fine watercolor painter of the School of 19th century English masters like Cotman and de Wint. I was spellbound by his technique. When I heard that he took a group of favored senior students outdoor painting every weekend, I begged to be allowed to join and was reluctantly allowed as I was the youngest. We painted in foul weather and fine. Often when all the other students had dropped out in mid-winter, John Hobbs and I would cycle out manfully into the ice and wet snow alone, often adding glycerin to our watercolors to prevent them from freezing. Nicholson was an unbending master of the medium of

watercolor. He poured scorn on abstract art and all fashionable art of the day, freeing me from such concerns to study what was before me, light and cloud shadows racing across a landscape. 'Look and paint and don't look back', he would say, and I did, feeling one with nature and the nature of watercolor, even though a war was raging in Europe and the night sky often filled with silent flashes from bombs dropped on the far off mainland. At fourteen I felt remote from war, concerning myself only with the joy of painting in watercolor and exploring my island in search of subject.

INTRODUCTION

8

The Isle of Man's only export is its people. In 1948, it was time for me and my family to leave for the new world. My father who was an actor started a theatrical touring company called naturally enough, THE NEW WORLD THEATRE COMPANY and for two years he, and a small cast of actors, brought Shakespeare via school bus to every one silo town in Canada. I settled in Brantford, Ontario and for the first time in my life was away from the sea, and wondered how I could paint this new sharp-focused land.

I looked at Canadian painting for a clue, knowing of course I would have to find my own way. The Group of Seven offered no answers for me, nothing in my background could prepare me to paint in such an opaque way, but Tom Thomson could paint light and David Milne could handle watercolor in a way with which I could identify. In 1951, Carl Schaeffer came to teach a summer school at the Doon School of Art at Doon in Ontario. This was my first opportunity to meet an artist who had succeeded in recreating the crisp strong line and color of the rural Ontario with which I was now familiar. Carl was a good influence on me at that time as well as being a great deal of fun. He was forever dressing up in a Confederate army uniform and charging up and down the rolling hills. When he was finally out of sight, we could hear the distant report of his muzzle-loading musket. I admired his watercolors greatly, as I still do today. He gave me a start in seeing what was for me a new land.

The early fifties were difficult economic times for me, there was little time for the pleasures of painting but long hours of work that dies with the worker. This was before the Canada Council and before commercial galleries. Before the wheel. No one but Vincent Massey bought art. Even David Milne was slowly dying from his poor sales. In one year, 1952, I painted only one watercolor.

In the spring of 1955, I moved to British Columbia. My wife Mary had died and I was left with two daughters, Lynn (two years old) and Jennifer (four years old). My father's NEW WORLD THEATRE COMPANY had run out of money and steam in Penticton in the beautiful Okanagan Valley. My parents invited me to come out west and start again. I firmly believe in running away, because it was after my arrival in Penticton that I once more had time to paint. I taught children's art classes and old ladies' art classes and in between I painted the Okanagan hills and lakes.

The two years I spent in the Okanagan Valley gave me time to reflect on my past and what I was going to do with my future. I had always thought of myself as an artist from early childhood. My father had wisely articled me to a local architect when we lived on the Isle of Man, out of fear I would cut off my ear and live off the family. At 27 in 1957, the time had come to decide whether my future was to be in art or architecture. The decision was made for me. Like a message from heaven I received a letter from Mexico to say I had won a scholarship from the Instituto Allende in San Miguel de Allende. It was all the excuse I needed. Even though I did not have enough money at the time to accept it, I would find a way. I had accumulated 250 odd watercolors over the years. I hired an auctioneer

and the Knights of Pythias Hall and sold them all for an average of $5.00 each netting $1,250.00. I was on my way. I packed my art supplies and my two daughters into my little MG TD sports car and headed for Mexico.

I had as much difficulty coming to terms with the Mexican landscape as I had when I arrived in Ontario nearly 10 years earlier. I saw Mexico as black and white with occasional screaming primary colours. Mexico is a very violent country to me. The mountains are unfriendly, rocky and pierce the sky, then plunge into dark canyons, following no prearranged pattern. I responded to this landscape like the chameleon, and did some of my most uncharacteristic watercolors. Many of these works were later torn up and destroyed, to become the material for my first collages.

Toni and Yukiko Onley
in their Vancouver home, 1981.

These collages were to be my preoccupation for the next four years taking me out of the landscape and into the studio. It was not until my year in London (1963-64) that I again started looking at watercolors. I visited the Prints and Drawings room at the British Museum one day every week and rediscovered my roots. Here were the great Nineteenth century watercolor painters of England I had so fervently tried to emulate as a boy. I was meeting them again like old friends, from a golden age. Little watercolors filled with light, space and spirit. I held them in my hands; Turner's, exploding with light, John Sell Cotman's solidly built compositions, building wash upon wash, and the loaded brush of David Cox. All my patron saints. I had come home to my source.

When I returned to Vancouver in 1964, I would climb down the ladder from my big works and reinvolve myself directly with my landscape. The new landscapes would be different, informed more by the compositional involvements of the minimal collages of the past three years. They are now abstract paintings that become landscapes in the doing. They are archetypal as well as particular, personal as well as universal images. But I am a northern temperament, at home drying my watercolors in the clear thin air of Arctic deserts, British Columbia's glacial lakes and coastal islands, Georgian Bay or Japan, whose spiritual paths I cross, and whose brushes I use.

I use a modern flying boat to take me to the most remote locations in search of my subjects. It's an update of Tom Thomson's canoe, and more far reaching. The watercolors in this book all come from my many flights along the B.C. Coast, up into the interior mountain lakes and across Canada to Georgian Bay, where for short periods each summer since 1972, I have painted watercolors with Canadian sculptor and fellow pilot Robert Murray, mooring our two airplanes in his little sheltered inlet on Lookout Island, his family's summer home. From here, armed with watercolors, paper and flyrods, we head out to range the islands, inlets and rivers of Georgian Bay. Lookout Island was also the stepping-off point for my 6000 mile Arctic flight of 1975.

After travelling the crowded earth, I come home to Canada and appreciate, time and time again, our great natural resource of space; the miles and miles of miles and miles. It's my cornucopia of subjects to paint without end. I drop in from the sky disturbing the silence only momentarily, then leaving the ancient land once more to converse with the sky. It's my home and all I need.

Our own parish is the only place we need when we would find subjects for our art; but we have to go round the world and enter our own parish anew from another side before we can see those subjects.
PAUL NASH, Letter 1937-38

PHOTO: IWAO MATSUO

Toni Onley
Vancouver, April 1981

white post, Lookout Island, pointe au Baril, ontario, July 20 1973   onley

'British Columbia is heaven. It trembles within me and pains with its wonder as when a child I first awakened to the song of the earth at home. Only the hills are bigger, the torrents are bigger. The sea is here, and the sky is vast; and humans – little bits of mind – clamber up rocky slopes, creep in and out of mountain passes, fish in the streams, build little hermit cabins in sheltered places, curl up in sleeping bags and sleep under the stars. The Japanese fish, Chinese have vegetable gardens, Hindoos haul wood, and I often feel that only the Chinese of the 11th and 12th century ever interpreted the spirit of such a country. We have not yet awakened to its nature.'
FREDERIC H. VARLEY[1]

PROLOGUE: TRADITIONS

Varley's statement upon his arrival on the West Coast in 1926 shows the artist's predicament when he finds himself surrounded by some of the most spectacular landscape in all of Canada. His comment that only the painters of the Sung dynasty in China could have interpreted the spirit of such a country is an indication of the problem facing all landscape painters before and since.

White Post, Lookout Island, Point-au-Baril, Ontario, July 20, 1973
'You can sometimes find interesting things to paint in the most unexpected places. I remember going into this little ravine on Lookout Island to get away from the wind of Georgian Bay. There was a small dead tree there and a little growing bush to one side. These elements appealed to me and my painting almost became a still life. I squared off the bushes for the sake of the arrangement.'

Like other artists before him such as Thomas Fripp (1864-1931) and Charles John Collings (1848-1931) who came to British Columbia, Varley had some knowledge of the British watercolor tradition. Until then, in fact, watercolor had been the medium most commonly used by landscape painters. Its application to the landscape of British Columbia was gradually supplanted by oil painting. Today, there are very few good landscape painters, and fewer watercolorists. Bringing watercolor and landscape together in a unique way is Toni Onley's very special achievement.

The British watercolor school of painting emerged in England at about the middle of the Eighteenth century when artists such as Paul Sandby (1730-1809) utilized water soluble pigments to color drawings, especially of a topographical nature. At this time, a classical system of landscape painting as seen in the work of Claude Lorrain in the previous century, was respected by all landscape artists and it was inevitable that the taking of topographical views would be rendered more artistic by making them more 'picturesque', or appropriate for a picture, one that was intended to evoke some form of aesthetic delight. In fact, the notion of an ideal landscape, partly imaginary, partly real, guided the artist's mind and hand.

One of the early theorists on both watercolor and landscape painting in Britain was Alexander Cozens, (1717-1786). In his A NEW METHOD OF LANDSCAPE (published c. 1785), Cozens made the following observation on landscape painting:

The originality of Cozens' work was that watercolors (or ink) were no longer used as an embellishment for an outline, but as painted forms applied quite directly to the paper and juxtaposed to one another in terms of light and shadow. The NEW METHOD put forward the notion of 'blotting' whereby the application of blots could suggest landscape for the artist's invention, just as well as nature could.

'Composing landscapes by invention, is not the art of imitating individual nature; it is more; it is forming artificial representations of landscape on the general principles of nature, founded in unity of character, which is true simplicity; concentrating in each individual composition the beauties, which judicious imitation would select from those which are dispersed in nature.'[2]

'To sketch in the common way, is to transfer ideas from the mind to the paper, or canvas, in outlines, in the slightest manner. To blot, is to make varied spots and shapes with ink on paper, producing accidental forms without lines, from which ideas are presented to the mind. This is conformable to nature, for in nature, forms are not distinguished by lines, but by shade and colour. To sketch is to delineate ideas; blotting suggests them.'[3]

By the early Nineteenth century, watercolor had begun to vie with oil painting in popularity, yet watercolors were always relegated to secondary places (if not hung completely out-of-sight) in the Academy exhibitions, as other drawings were. Reacting to this, watercolor artists formed their own Societies to foster the appreciation of watercolor and to organize public exhibitions exclusively of watercolor paintings. The scale of the works increased, and their elaborate frames emulated those of many oil paintings.

These societies and their exhibitions firmly established the art of watercolor in British art, unlike anywhere else in Europe. Some artists continued to paint in both oils and watercolors, while others specialized in the watercolor medium.

There soon emerged a number of artists whose mastery of the medium, combined with the inspiration they derived from the British landscape, made of them artists of great significance. Among them were Alexander Cozens' son, John Robert Cozens (1752-1797), John Sell Cotman (1782-1842), David Cox (1783-1859) and Peter de Wint (1784-1849). The watercolors of Joseph Mallord William Turner (1775-1851) transcended everything that had been done before him.

By the beginning of this century, many British artists continued to use the medium and watercolor was very much a part of artistic training in the British Isles. It is no surprise, then, to find a young artist on the Isle of Man in the 1940's called Toni Onley taking instruction in watercolor from John Hobbs Nicholson, a man steeped in the great tradition of the Nineteenth century. At a time when many art schools had abandoned a curriculum based on techniques in favor of more 'creative' or self-expressive ideals (when not oriented towards commercial art), Onley was uniquely fortunate to be taught the very fine and very difficult technique of watercolor.

Within the context of British watercolor, two principal tendencies may be identified. The first, as exemplified by the works of Sandby is solidly based on draughtsmanship – the idea is transferred from the mind to paper in outlines, as Alexander Cozens mentioned. The second tendency, as exhibited in the works of Cozens, Cotman and Turner depends less on drawing than on tonal arrangements of shapes, facilitating the use of more or less broad washes of color. The first tendency is far more literal in its rendering of landscape, the second is far more interpretative of nature, and leads to greater experimentation in terms of what watercolor can do. Even in the Twentieth century, artists have generally worked in one way or the other, and often in both.

For landscape painting, the extreme portability of the medium renders it most practical for work directly from nature. Apart from pigments in cakes or small tubes, a mixing tray, a brush and paper, the only other necessity is water. Watercolor is direct and immediate, most suitable to the capturing of 'impressions' of nature, and quick-drying. Such advantages explain why the medium remains popular for landscape painters, at least with those who are not afraid of the medium's difficulty.

These factors, along with the British origin or training of many of Canada's most significant painters, explain why watercolor is so important to our painting and its development.

The tradition of watercolor painting in Canada was well established in the Nine-teenth century. A cursory review of the catalogs of the society exhibitions in Toronto and Montreal from the 1870's to World War 1 shows its importance. Even before then, such artists as Thomas Davies (1737-1812), George Heriot (1766-1844) and James Cockburn (1778-1847), the latter two students of Paul Sandby at Woolwich, had used watercolor to record the topography and the general features of the New Land. Professional artists such as Daniel

Fowler (1810-1894), Lucius O'Brien (1832-1899), John A. Fraser (1838-1898), F.M. Bell-Smith (1846-1923) and Robert F. Gagen (1847-1926) exhibited their watercolors of Canadian land-scapes from the Atlantic to the Pacific.

After the Great War, a number of Canadian artists continued to paint in watercolor. They formed the Canadian Society of Painters in Watercolor in 1926. Such painters as Fred Brigden (1871-1956), C.W. Jefferies (1869-1951), Franklin Carmichael (1890-1945), A.J. Casson (b.1898), Walter J. Phillips (1884-1963) and Carl Schaeffer (b.1903) were

all very active in the medium and have produced some of Canada's most significant watercolors.

It is in this general context that one may con-sider the watercolors of Toni Onley. As Canadian watercolors, they are a culmination of sorts – the most significant work done in the medium today, and this, for a variety of reasons.

Varley's statement about Chinese painters of the 11th and 12th centuries interpreting such a country as British Columbia provides us with some of these reasons. The statement is in one

sense a brilliant perception of how the landscape could best be interpreted. But taken literally, it is not altogether appropriate. The Chinese paint-ers did not interpret any specific landscape in their paintings, rather an 'idea' of a landscape was painted. The fact that many Chinese landscape paintings are evocative to us of the clouds and mists of the West Coast shows how universal that 'idea' was and is.

The British Columbian landscape reminded Varley of certain Chinese paintings. The land-scape was somehow 'oriental', as many others have observed since then. Plum trees bloom, bamboo grows as well as tall pines, suggesting a similarity in climate with the Orient. It is inevitable that the landscape and the vegetation on the West Coast should suggest to artists that vision of landscape across the Pacific Ocean. Standing on Long Beach near Tofino, the horizon naturally beckons, and this attraction to Asia is almost a natural aspiration.

But there are many oceans between.

John H. Nicholson
River Glass, Tromode, Isle of Man, 1946.
Watercolor on paper 33.6 x 46.5 cm

This watercolor was painted at the time Toni Onley was one of his students.

14

Chinese painting at the time of the Sung dynasty was already the high point of a long tradition. As early as the Fifth century, a writer named Hsieh Ho set forth Six Canons of painting. These canons or basic principles also provided criteria for a very special aesthetic, very different from the aesthetic developed in Western civilization. Only within the past hundred years or so have the concerns of Oriental painters influenced Western art. Such influences are very much in evidence in the watercolors of Toni Onley. A brief discussion of the Chinese aesthetic will enhance one's appreciation of these very special watercolors.

The Six Canons have been respected by Chinese painters for about fifteen centuries, with more or less emphasis given to one canon or another according to the ages and the artists themselves. Certainly the most important seems to have been 'spirit resonance', a concept that is very difficult for Westerners to appreciate fully. It is somewhat akin to capturing the Tao in art, the universal principle, nature itself, which includes the harmony of opposing forces, and could only be achieved through meditation and contemplation. Such a sense of harmony with the universe combined with proficiency on the technical level, also acquired through meditation, study and practice, was a prerequisite to artistic excellence.

The concept of 'spirit resonance' was made manifest in such qualities as 'naturalness' (as opposed to naturalism), effortlessness, a respect for the universal principles of nature, a concern for the inherent structure in whatever was being depicted, pictorial reality (not realism), a concern for seasonal aspect and mood, evidence of a life-movement or growth and a healthy respect for tradition and the past. All these qualities had to

be conveyed by the best possible (and appropriate) brushwork, and the most skillful use of color, or more usually ink.

The Chinese 'landscape' was a 'mountain and sea' picture. It encompassed opposite elements, it sought to convey the TAO, and the notion of infinity was very much present. In addition, while the vertical format of the hanging scroll, or the square album-leaf painting, had two dimensions,

the traditional handscroll added the element of time: as the scroll was unrolled, the viewer's eye travelled along it, much as it would over a panoramic or all-encompassing landscape. Such paintings were never viewed all at once, but only a portion at a time, within the distance between both arms engaged in rolling and unrolling the painting.

Toni Onley. 1966
Untitled Sumi; Ink on paper. 28 x 35.1 cm

In a culture where writing consists of ideograms, good calligraphy was of paramount importance and had a major influence on painting. Much of the basis of an understanding of Chinese painting lies in the appreciation of the brushwork, the vehicle that gives shape and 'bone' to any picture – and thereby allows it to reach the essential 'spirit resonance' ideal.

Such a subtle and rather ineffable aesthetic is acquired with considerable difficulty by Westerners. One example of the difference in attitude and approach is indicated by the fact that Western artists have traditionally used the human figure or 'life drawing' for their apprenticeship, while Chinese painters spend years mastering the fine art of painting plum blossoms, bamboo and pine trees in pursuit of the elusive 'spirit resonance', a very different ideal than our traditional ideals of realism, naturalism and self-expression. Such concepts were of secondary importance to the Chinese in their quest of 'spirit resonance' through meditation rather than imitation. Meditation enhanced any direct observation of nature.

The introduction of Buddhism to China was to have a considerable impact on the traditional (Taoist) art. Buddhism did not conflict with Taoism, stressing as it did that enlightenment could be reached through meditation. The Ch'an sect (or Zen) held that enlightenment was revealed by sudden flashes of insight. Ch'an painters, who were often monks, inevitably used quick, powerful brushwork and brief, expressive areas of wash to record the essential nature of such insights, which 'required the most careful and assiduous training, psychological as well as technical, because the brush-strokes became reflections from the mind transmitted by the skill of the hand.'[4] Sung dynasty painters like Mi Fei, Mu Ch'i and Yü Chien were superb practitioners of the style, and one may suppose that it was their abbreviated, atmospheric and 'essential' landscapes that Varley thought most appropriate to the landscape of British Columbia.

The spontaneity of the 'Ch'an' method can only rarely be achieved by Western artists since 'no painter who did not possess a full command of the technical means could ever transmit such fleeting glimpses or momentary reflections from a realm beyond sensual perception. The brush had to respond instantaneously and unremittingly to the pulse-beat of the creative soul; the material labor had to be reduced to a minimum, a few strokes or splashes which could serve to reawaken the vision in the beholder's mind.'[5]

Four centuries later, in the early Ch'ing dynasty, an eccentric monk-painter named Chu Ta (known as Pa-ta-Shan-Jên) used this style in thousands of paintings. Like the paintings of his Sung dynasty predecessors, his were the result of a simple and direct contact with nature. All these painters share one characteristic – their preference for a 'boneless' or 'lineless' technique, their brushwork being something between a wash and a scumble rather than carefully drawn lines.

The significance of such work to Toni Onley could not have been more auspiciously brought home to him than during the recent (1978) one-man exhibition of his prints and watercolors at the National Historic Museum in Taipei (Taiwan).

The experience was a memorable one, related here by the artist:

The 'boneless' or 'lineless' painting technique used by Pa-Ta-Shan-Jên (and his Sung predecessors) can be kept in mind when considering Alexander Cozens' 'blots', which were meant to suggest nature more effectively than a line drawing could. The difference was that the 'blots' or spirited washes in Cozens' paintings were based on the observation of lights and shadows in nature. The Chinese painters used their spirited brush strokes to capture and convey 'spirit resonance' or that essential spirit, something that has more to do with landscape and painting in themselves than any attempt at imitating nature. By 'recreating' a landscape in their paintings, the Chinese often were much truer to nature and its forces which they understood through meditation as well as observation.

It is interesting to note that before 'forming a blot', Cozens admonishes his reader: 'Possess your mind strongly with a subject', later continuing:

The difference between Cozens and the Chinese painter is that the latter does not 'make all possible variety of shapes and strokes' on the paper, but only those which are required to convey 'spirit resonance' or the essential nature of the subject. To be fair to Cozens,

'In the next gallery, completely by chance, there was an exhibition of SHUMO (ink and water paintings) by my Chinese patron saint, Pa-ta-Shan-Jên, poet, prince, monk, drunkard and painter of 1,000 paintings for each year of his 85 year life. His fish, flowers, trees and rocks all appear to be conversing with each other. At the hands of a lesser artist they would be reduced to mere caricatures. But Pa-Ta-Shan-Jên has breathed life into his subjects that speak to me from across the ages. I could feel his presence from the Ch'ing dynasty sitting in the room, tippling sake for inspiration. Somehow his presence made all the bother of mounting this show of mine worthwhile.'[6]

'Take a camel's hair brush, as large as can be conveniently used, dip it in a mixture of drawing ink and water, which must be of such a degree of lightness as will best suit your purpose, and with the swiftest hand make all possible variety of shapes and strokes upon your paper, confining the disposition of the whole to the general subject in your mind.'[7]

however, it should be pointed out that his 'new method of landscape' was a means that would enable a painter to invent landscape subjects. When this development had been achieved, better perception and greater facility in rendering nature – the ultimate goal – could be attained.

In their own way, the watercolors of Toni Onley begin to reconcile the aesthetics of the West and the East – in the spirit of the TAO – and in the spirit of the landscape of British Columbia. They 'awaken us to its nature' in a manner and through a medium which Varley might not have expected. Their spirit is the spirit of the artist and this, ultimately, goes beyond the particularities of any geographic region.

Rock, Jordon River, N.S. August 8 1974   Onley

BECOMING

'Do not grasp the brush before the spirit and the thoughts are concentrated. The ideas must all be in the eye before they are carried out with the brush; afterwards they may be developed in accordance with the style (rules); and then it may be said, that what is grasped by the mind is expressed by the hand.' HAN CHO, c. 1121[12]

Rock, Jordan River, Nova Scotia, August 8, 1974

'In '74, while waiting for the departure of the Icebreaker 'Louis St. Laurent' which was to take me to the Arctic, I found I had time to kill because of the delays. So I rented a car and drove around Nova Scotia. One day, I was driving over a bridge and noticed the river bed of the Jordan River. The water was very low, and there were the great boulders there. I don't know how they got there. I parked the car, went down to the riverbed and did this watercolor of one of those strange boulders. Later I made a print of the subject which had such strong appeal for me.'

A teacher, who was eager to point out the error in the watercolor of a seven-petalled daffodil painted in his first year of school, was perhaps confusing to a budding artist. Even then, he knew instinctively that a painting of a flower is very different from the flower itself. A painting was something you made up from what you had seen or imagined. The painting done during the holidays at Ramsey was like that: full-rigged ships were not too often found in the little harbour, but they were the most important part of the stories told by his grandfather, a retired sailing-ship captain.

Later at the Douglas School of Art, Toni Onley spent some time copying the BOOK OF KELLS, and learning to paint what was set before him, learning the theory and conventions of perspective. Success hinged on whether the picture looked convincing or not. That was truth to Nature.

The lessons in landscape taught by John Hobbs Nicholson were the watercolor paintings he did. He was a successful young painter, and people liked to join him on his sketching trips. A fourteen-year-old Toni Onley was no exception. He wanted to accompany Nicholson and learn all there was to learn about painting because the curriculum of the School did not teach him much about it, and probably less about art. Much more was to be learned when he compared his watercolor to that which had been executed by Nicholson.

This apprenticeship, if one may call it that, lasted about four years. Many hours were spent sketching with Nicholson in all kinds of weather, fair and foul. Lessons were not always pleasant as Nicholson was quite a taskmaster. On the first outing to Rushen Abbey, the group sketched Monk's Bridge. Nicholson came to where Toni was painting, after a time, and noticed the new paint-box. One by one, he picked the new tubes of paint from the box. When the pigment was not permanent enough or if he had a particular dislike for the color, he chucked it into the river. Toni Onley protested that he could have returned the offending colors, exchanging them for better pigments. Nicholson answered that Onley would now remember the inferior pigments forever, and should be grateful for the lesson. The pigments were Hooker's Green Light, Gamboge, Carmine, Chrome Yellow, Vandyke Brown, Sap Green and Chinese White.

The addition of Chinese White to any color renders the pigment opaque. Such use of 'body color' is not tolerated by orthodox practitioners of the fine art of watercolor, whose essential attribute, they maintain, is its transparency. White in watercolor is the white of the paper. This means that any object appearing white will be left as unpainted paper. Some painters would achieve other highlights by scratching the damp paper, removing the painted surface. White clouds or snow present interesting difficulties for painters, since the medium requires that one work from light to dark: the clouds or snow would not be painted, except for their grey or blue shadows. The behaviour of the medium, the interaction of wet paper and pigment, present further difficulties. Control and mastery of the medium meant that all these factors became predictable, and the competent watercolorist could carry out his design within (or in spite of) the medium's limitations.

The tradition that Nicholson imparted to his students was based on landscape. It was the artist's duty to represent the beauties of nature in as convincing a way as possible, through good design or composition and sound technique.

One of the accepted conventions was the use of foreground, middle-ground and background, usually in receding colors. The humid atmosphere in the British Isles made this possible as the landscape became lighter when it is seen through more and more haze. Colors were more intense (usually darker) as they approached the foreground. A painting was very much like the view through a window, the edges of the paper being the equivalent of the window frame, through which a third dimension, depth, was to be created.

But the picture, to be convincing, needed more than depth. The viewer had to be content with what was contained in the frame, and this is where application of compositional principles was important. A golden mean of sorts was recommended. It suggested that the most important elements of the composition, such as centres of interest, or the horizon, should generally occur along the imaginary lines dividing the height and width of the paper into thirds. The horizon, for instance, should be about a third of the way up the picture, or two-thirds of the way up. Nicholson once had his students construct 'view-finders' as a guide to their compositions. This was a cardboard frame with thread lines occurring at the dividing thirds, both horizontally and vertically.

The premise of landscape painting in the British Isles was the love of country and an interest in the weather. Much as the Dutch artists of the Seventeenth century, such as Ruysdael and Hobbema had done before them, English artists delighted in painting views. These could be made more 'picturesque' by the application of formulae for the less gifted artists. Great artists created their own as it suited them, and these would soon become codified by the less-gifted. The Romantics' love of Nature sent artists outdoors to paint or to sketch, but much excellent painting continued to be elaborated in the studio from sketches or from memory. The great Turner usually worked at his watercolors in his studio at night by lamplight. His attitude can best be exemplified by the story, often repeated, of a lady who was offended by his liberties and declared to him on seeing one of his sunsets: 'I never saw such colors in a sunset', to which Turner replied: 'Madame, don't you wish you could?'

By the late Nineteenth century, however, most artists worked in nature, out-of-doors, taking sketches of views which interested them, often finishing them on the spot, or elaborating a larger composition from them in the studio later, where greater control was possible.

Nicholson finished his sketches on the spot. His personal technique was based on a pencil sketch where important areas were sketched in. Then, the principal washes would be laid and details picked out in brush-point. He had a very effective dry brush technique where he would drag a brush loaded with partially dry pigment over his favored textured paper. When he and Toni Onley were out sketching together, Nicholson would never allow his student to sit too close to him. In this way, the student had to meet his own difficulties and solve his own problems, be that color-mixing, the application of a wash or the lay-out of a composition.

The lessons were effective because, like the tubes of pigment thrown into Rushen River, much of his teaching was contained in a critique after the student had finished his painting. Late in 1945 or early in 1946, after the port of Liverpool was opened to visitors to see the destruction of war-time bombing raids, Nicholson took his sketching group over for almost a week. Toni Onley recalls one lesson in particular. After laboring over a watercolor of what was left of a submarine basin for a couple of hours, Nicholson took one look at it and with one stroke of heavy pencil drew a horizon right across the painting, where the principles of perspective suggested it should be. Lessons in perspective of a theoretical nature learned at art school had to become 'second-nature' and were to be applied intuitively.

The weekends spent sketching with Nicholson made Toni Onley aware of the light, cloud, fog and mist that often enshrouded the Isle of Man, and under Nicholson's guidance, he soon made good progress as a landscape painter. Success on the Isle of Man was having one's pictures shown in a framing shop in Douglas. When Toni Onley's were, he was seventeen years old. Nicholson had little time for him after that.

Even after Toni Onley was apprenticed to a local architect, he continued to paint in watercolor by himself. He now became much influenced by the work of other painters, such as Samuel Palmer and the emphasis became one of design and the search for a personal style. His only exposure to the work of other artists was through magazines and books. He found works by some contemporary British artists fascinating even though he found he had little sympathy for them. Nothing in his education prepared him to accept the obvious breaks with tradition in John Piper's watercolors, and in those of Graham Sutherland.

Above: Toni Onley. Freighter and Tug, Mersey River, 1945. Watercolor on paper, 27.9 x 38.1 cm.

Left: Toni Onley. Old Shipyard, Isle of Man, 1946. Watercolor on paper, 28.5 x 38 cm.

The Onley family immigrated into Canada in 1948. There was more interest than time for artistic pursuits. The new country was unsympathetic to Onley and he realized how, in Brantford, Ontario, he missed the sea. He found little time to paint. He visited exhibitions in Toronto at the Art Gallery of weekends and saw how Canadian painters had painted the country. Paintings by the Group of Seven interested him, but he had little sympathy for (and less experience with) the opaque medium of oil paint. The watercolors of David Milne were of great interest to him, as were those of Carl Schaeffer.

In 1949, he married Mary Burrows, another artist he had met on a brief visit to the Doon School of Art. He attended the School for about 10 days during a vacation in 1951, with Carl Schaeffer as the principal instructor. Toni's strong inclination towards design made itself manifest in his work at that time. The artist imposed an 'order' on the subject, influenced by the design styles he emulated. But there was too little time for painting. First he worked for a land surveyor, then for Cockshutt Farm Equipment as a designer, then for a commercial art firm in Hamilton called Standard Engravers. After his wife's sudden death in 1955, he moved to Penticton with his two daughters. His parents had settled there.

Now there was more time to paint. He soon was employed teaching art classes on Saturdays, allowing him all week to paint the Okanagan landscape. He painted more than he had in Ontario. But more part-time work for an overworked architect soon became full-time work, once again removing him from his painting. He had applied for a scholarship to attend the Art Institute at San Miguel de Allende and when he found out he was successful, he had 250 of his watercolors auctioned and was off to Mexico for three years.

The watercolors he had done in Ontario and in Penticton were the result of his interest in contemporary British painters such as Ben Nicholson. The landscape became a scheme for his design. A work such as PENTICTON of 1957, shows how forms derived from landscape could be transformed into a decorative scheme, with colors used sparingly. The forms are accentuated by a line, as if etched.

As landscape, Mexico was unsympathetic and almost bewildering. Toni Onley soon tired of the schematic landscape designs. He questioned everything he had done so far. Frustrated, and in an uncharacteristic display of temperament, he tore up all his watercolors, letting the pieces drop to the floor. The pieces created their own patterns, new different patterns, as if design could also be spontaneous, without preconception. Toni Onley picked up on that idea.

Artistic environments are stimulating: the discussions within a lively community of artists, the time and the freedom to paint, everything led to a complete re-evaluation of his work. Destroying the old watercolors was very much a part of that process. It would be almost seven years before he would do watercolors again.

The dominant influence now was the group of Abstract Expressionist painters of New York. The patterns that emerged from the shreds of watercolors were preserved, and the collages that were the result were the first time that a new response to the work was made evident. Forms could suggest themselves, as well as be deliberately created, like patterns emerging from blots. A dialogue was possible. Random patterns could be selected, and stuck to paper, with new patterns emerging, a result of the artist's sense of natural order. From these harmonious arrangements of forms and shapes, he became aware that the collages could be further reduced and simplified to only those elements which were essential. It was a further effort to divest himself of almost everything he had learned until then. The collages or paintings themselves taught all the lessons that mattered.

The practice and experience of AbstractExpressionism was beneficial in many ways. It was the first step in a 'cleansing' process and a rediscovery. The movement, a child of Surrealism, rebels against the tyranny of subject matter: everything in the painting was now 'about' itself. Canvas and the arrangement of pigments, or (perhaps more accurately) their application was the only subject matter. The use of the word 'picture' became meaningless. The works were usually on a large scale. Nothing on the surface could refer to anything that might tend to negate that surface, such as an area of a blue which could be seen as deeper space, or that third dimension which painters since the Renaissance had sought to achieve. The painter was to free himself from any preconceptions of what a painting should be. In this way, he would concentrate on the process of painting itself. The source was the unconscious, and to facilitate its release, artists introduced the element of chance into their paintings. Max Ernst, the Surrealist, had even used a process called 'decalcomania', a method requiring the painting of two canvases, their pressing together and peeling apart. The patterns created were used as the starting points for paintings. Other painters used 'automatism', a technique which required letting the brush move freely on the canvas according to the artist's subconscious.

Such painters had long forgotten Alexander Cozens' 'blots' in the late Eighteenth century: 'To blot, is to make varied spots and shapes with ink on paper, producing accidental forms without lines, from which ideas are presented to the mind.'[8]

With its concern for surface and paint, Abstract Expressionism placed a new value in the brush-stroke and brushwork. The movement of the brush recorded the painting process, which was the only subject. Such concerns inevitably lead to Chinese and Japanese art, where calligraphy is the most important art form of all.

The first important works by Toni Onley emerged, and it is through these oils and collages that he first achieved some form of public notoriety at a one-man exhibition at the Vancouver Art Gallery in the late fall of 1958.

He returned to Vancouver in 1960, still searching, still working up large abstract compositions, using collage and acrylics. Watercolor was still the furthest thing away from his mind. Landscape was perhaps further still.

In 1963, a Canada Council grant took him to London, England. This trip was an attempt to find something about himself, and one way of doing this was to see what his reactions were to the artists he had once admired so much: Cotman, Cox, de Wint and Turner. He met these artists in the Prints and Drawings Room at the British Museum. Every Thursday afternoon, for several weeks, he would go through box after box of great English watercolors. He idly thought that it would be interesting to go back to the

landscape again, but the notion was put aside, and he continued to work on his large abstract works, toying with watercolor now and then, but studying various printmaking techniques. He had discovered one thing: he still loved the watercolors he saw and recognized a feeling within him of somehow 'belonging' to this tradition. He returned to Vancouver in 1964.

In 1965, while working on an acrylic painting, the various elements of the composition seemed to require further definition of the space they

occupied. In a flash, breaking the rule of Abstract Expressionism, he painted a line across the canvas, as if behind the forms, suggesting the forbidden depth. The painting had become a landscape. This was CHALK FIELD of 1965.

He was now free to turn his thoughts directly to landscape, with a new-found freedom. Landscape elements now suggested form to him, and such elements, reduced to their essential shapes, became a new source for the making of paintings.

The purchase, one day, in Vancouver's Chinatown, of a large goat-hair brush and some Sumi ink led to further experimentation. Turning now to this very liquid but very expressive medium, he discovered once again the magic of the brush, ink and paper the Chinese had used for centuries. Fellow artist Chin Chêk Lam gave him paper which he thought appropriate for Onley's use. Many of the Sumi ink paintings were simple compositional arrangements of shapes, almost like still-life, others were frankly landscape.

In 1966-67, appointed painting instructor at the University of Victoria for that term, he noticed an advertisement about flying lessons and a guarantee of a pilot's license for $500. Having some time to spare, he took lessons, got the pilot's license and soon purchased his own plane. By 1968, he was flying around the Gulf Islands to small landing strips or landing his plane on the hard sand beaches of the West Coast of Vancouver Island, painting watercolor landscapes once again. But the landscape this time was quite abstract, informed as it was by almost ten years of non-figurative work.

Toni Onley (right) is seen here painting with fellow artist and friend Robert Murray.

PHOTO: CINTRA LOFTING MURRAY

21

Lookout Island, Georgian Bay, July 26 1976 (i/ii)   Onley

Lookout Island, Georgian Bay, July 26, 1976

'This is what you see looking West from Murray's Inlet, a strange reflection of the rock there. There is also a little bush on a peninsula. That intense black line is a chunk of pigment that dried on the brush. I'm always delighted when I find that some pigment has dried into my brush. This seems to happen because my brush always goes to the bottom of my paint box where the Black is. The stroke with the black was painted in first, and the rest of the painting was more or less determined by that brushstroke and some of the elements in the landscape.'

'He who deliberates and moves the brush intent upon making a picture, misses to a still greater extent the art of painting, while he who cogitates and moves the brush without such intentions, reaches the art of painting. His hands will not get stiff; his heart will not grow cold; without knowing how, he accomplishes it.' CHANG-YEN-YÜAN, C. 845 [9]

A BRUSH WITH SPIRIT

The new watercolor landscapes are now a way of life. As often as he can, time and weather permitting, armed with his watercolor box, goat hair brush, his Winsor and Newton paints and Arches paper, he flies in search of subject. When he returns home towards evening, he usually has painted up to five or six watercolors. The watercolors keep growing in number paralleling people's interest in them.

Flying small planes in search of landscape subjects precludes the possibility of large, cumbersome equipment. Toni Onley has devised a paint box made out of birch plywood reinforced with steel brackets at the bottom corners. Closed, it measures 41 by 42 centimeters, and is seven centimeters high. It weighs about three kilograms. It divides into two compartments: a large compartment holds paper, about 50 sheets of quarter imperial size, that is about 30 by 39 centimeters. These are cut from full imperial size sheets (56 by 76 centimeters) or more frequently from the larger 'jumbo' size sheets (80 by 120 centimeters) which yield eight quarter imperial sheets. The paper he prefers is a smooth Velin Arches rag paper. His paper is not as heavily sized as most English-made papers, and has just the right absorbency for his particular technique. Some watercolors are done on 'David Cox' paper, a toned paper favored by many watercolor painters in the late Nineteenth and the early part of this century, but which is no longer manufactured. Toni Onley found two quires (50 imperial sheets) in a Victoria art supply shop, which the owner was more than happy to sell at a great discount.

The other half of the paint box reveals a small compartment for tubes of pigment being used – Winsor and Newton, of course. (Boxes of spare pigments are stored in another compartment, on the paper storage side of the box.) There are three other compartments, the bottom of each consisting of concave pieces of plastic (from a fluorescent light fixture). This plastic has been finely sanded to hold water without beading. In one compartment, dabs of pigment squirted from the tubes are found, requiring only a freshening of water to release their colors. The other two compartments, or shallow troughs, are used as mixing trays. A roll of librarian's tape and the big Chinese goat hair brush complete the equipment. Fresh water is carried in an unbreakable jug, some of which is poured into a large wide-mouthed container for cleaning the brush or picking up water. Nothing else is needed. The box comes apart at the hinges and one side becomes the drawing board. The sheet of paper is taped to its back or lid.

Toni Onley's palette at this time consists of the following colors:

French Ultramarine	Raw Sienna
Winsor Blue	Burnt Sienna
Cobalt Blue	Brown Madder (Alizarin)
Antwerp Blue	Alizarin Crimson
Winsor Green	Light Red
Yellow Ochre	Cadmium Yellow
Raw Umber	Cadmium Red
Burnt Umber	Sepia
	Lamp Black

French Ultramarine is an indispensable color to Toni. It can be used with a variety of colors to produce very rich grays. For instance, the admixture of Sepia to French Ultramarine will produce a very rich gray, or as Toni calls it, a West Coast gray, while the admixture of Light Red will produce a slightly more opaque pearly gray.

Winsor Blue is Winsor and Newton's name for phthalocyanine blue, a deep intense blue with a slight green tint to it. It is a very strong color and one that Toni has used since childhood. The admixture of Burnt Sienna will produce a brownish green or olive color. Winsor Blue is also a good color for rendering water, but it is too intense to be used in its pure state, and is usually mixed.

Cobalt Blue is a very gentle blue and is a good sky color. It is a color that Toni sometimes uses in its pure state. It too will produce beautiful grays, such as a very clean silvery gray when mixed with Light Red.

Antwerp Blue has been used by Toni since 1976. That summer, when he was at Emma Lake, in Saskatchewan, a student presented the color to him, saying 'Toni, I think this is 'your' color,' and he has used it ever since. Its slight greenish tint makes it very versatile as a color for rendering water, and it produces its own grays.

Winsor Green is a phthalocyanine green, the only green in Toni's palette. It is more versatile than the Viridian which he used in his youth, and is another indispensable color. In a pure state it is a very intense color. The admixture of Alizarin Crimson will produce a dirtier gray green (less intense) while another range of grays can be created by combining Alizarin Crimson and French Ultramarine to it.

Yellow Ochre is one of the oldest colors known to man. It will produce beautifully pale greens when mixed with the blues. With the admixture of Lamp Black, it will create beautiful browns, the color of wet sand. It is a more lively color than Raw Umber which it almost resembles.

Raw Umber has a grayish tinge to it. With French Ultramarine, it will produce a very beautiful gray, while a muddy green can be created when mixed with Winsor Blue. Another scale of greens is also possible when it is added to Winsor Green.

Burnt Umber will produce a very intense bottle green, when mixed with Winsor Green, while a deep gray can be produced when it is used with French Ultramarine.

Raw Sienna is a color similar to a dark ochre but is far more transparent. Its admixture to any gray will warm it considerably. When Lamp Black is added, a good sand color is rendered.

Burnt Sienna is another good color for producing greens and grays. Used with Winsor Blue and Winsor Green, it will produce an interesting scale of greens, while a deep stormy gray is produced by mixing it with French Ultramarine.

Brown Madder is an alizarin color, beautifully transparent. With Winsor Green, it will also produce an intense bottle green. It can also be used with Winsor Blue for rich blue and gray tones.

Alizarin Crimson is one of Toni's favored colors and he uses it often. It is strong but beautifully transparent and has the rather unusual characteristic of 'separating' from other colors with which it is mixed, much like Cobalt Violet, as its crystals rise to the surface. It is very useful for reducing the intensity of other colors, such as the greens and blues. When it is mixed with Winsor Blue, it creates beautiful grayish greens.

Light Red is an earth color, and is used almost exclusively for making grays, but can also be used mixed with Winsor Green to render it mossy; a gritty green, somewhat like a dry olive green.

Cadmium Red is used very occasionally when a very pure silver gray is required, a result of the admixture of Cobalt Blue.

Cadmium Yellow can also be used on rare occasions when the admixture of Antwerp Blue yields a very clear light green.

Sepia is a color that Toni had not used for several years, but now uses again. It is very soluble and is almost like a warm black, very useful in 'knocking down' colors or muting their harsh intensity. It produces the richest of dark greens when mixed with Winsor Green or the stormiest of grays when mixed with French Ultramarine.

Lamp Black was a pigment that John Hobbs Nicholson did not allow students to use, stating that it demonstrated a lack of will and a lack of invention. Black was to be produced by mixing French Ultramarine with Burnt Sienna. But the black that is so produced is inadequate: it is really not black at all, but a rich gray. Lamp Black is used to darken other colors, to give them a depth that is present when all light is absorbed. Lamp Black also seems to crystalize or suspend tiny particles of pigment in a wash and has a very special beauty. Another range of greens is produced when it is mixed with Winsor Green. It generally changes or reduces the intensity of other colors, such as blues.

The goat hair brush (or 'fude') which Toni Onley has now been using for several years is a very special brush. It is a Chinese brush and is much larger, fatter and longer than an ordinary watercolor brush. When purchased, a goat hair brush (available in many sizes) is very stiff, as the hairs are held together by a dry starch. Chinese or Japanese painters will usually soften the tip to the width required by their brush stroke or calligraphy. Onley's brush is softened completely. When wet, this brush can be brought to a point with a flick of the wrist. It is capable of holding a great deal of water or pigment. If its water is removed, it can also absorb water or pigment off the paper. It has a versatility which no other brush has.

This brush is very durable and takes much rough treatment. The artist can twist it, turn it, scrub the paper with it. It is most responsive to the artist who knows its ways. It is very different from the traditional sable watercolor brushes Onley once used and which he described:

'stiff sable for painting stiff, preconceived works, while Chinese brushes, made from goat hair, are soft, pliable, and hold a great quantity of color and water. They produce surprising spontaneous effects that the artist can respond to; with these big floppy brushes, the artist can creat a dialogue between himself and his work as it unfolds before him. Life and death, success or failure, the work demanding his total attention. The brush transmuted into an extension of his will.'[10]

To this description could be added the following advice by the Chinese writer on painting Kuo-Jo-hsü, who wrote in Sung dynasty times:

'The brush must be nimble, move swiftly in a continuous and connecting manner, so that the flow of life is not interrupted as the thoughts precede the brush. But the brush is also in the thoughts, and when the picture is finished, all the thoughts are there, and the image corresponds completely to the spirit. When the painter is inwardly serene, when his spirit is at ease and his thoughts calm, the mind is not exhausted and the brush not restrained.'[11]

There is a very large goat hair brush for Sumi ink drawings. There are thinner, longer Japanese calligraphy brushes. There are strange brushes which are entirely made from a stick of bamboo, the fibres of one extremity pounded until the woodfibre forms individual 'hairs' . . . a brush that has a very scratchy, very expressive, almost primitive character. There is one strange brush which is actually about eight small brushes whose bamboo or reed handles are bound in a row, so as to create a wide band of wash. One brush is made from feathers. These are specialty brushes, for specific purposes, requiring specific responses, and are not ordinarily carried in the paint box.

The goat hair brushes Toni Onley uses for his watercolors are very special to him and, when they wear out, are not disposed of lightly. In an occasional private ritual, the artist will bring the old and new brushes to the landscape. He will work with one or both. The old brush is left in the landscape, under a rock or in a log or tree. The brush is returned to nature from whence it came. In his way, Toni Onley parallels an old Japanese custom (fude-zuku) of burying brushes with ceremony in a special 'brush grave'.

The palette of colors, the use of such brushes, and the response of the artist to the landscape and to his materials are the elements of the watercolors in this book. Such a palette, when the choice of pigments is almost entirely oriented towards a range of grays, greens, gray-greens, blues and gray-blues is appropriate for the Canadian landscape, and specifically for the landscape of the West Coast. It is a landscape of personal choice for Toni Onley. There is no intensity of color in nature, with the exception of the presence (all too rare for some) of Cobalt Blue skies and Antwerp Blue seas, and the greens of a very verdant nature. The mists, fog, cloud and rain subdue color, filter it until it is an infinitely varying gray and green or gray and blue. Moreover, these harmonious dark colors of the West Coast, as if starved for light, seem to absorb it constantly, reflecting none. Everything is velvety. The landscape envelops. All the lakes and the ocean seem bottomless. There is water and high treed mountains everywhere. These often appear almost flat, with little modulation, receding planes of green or blue, according to distance and the light of day. Watercolor seems to have a particular affinity for such a landscape, but the medium requires an artist who will respond to it and to that landscape in a direct and intimate way.

Toni Onley no longer owns a sable brush, but his brush collection is very extensive, and they are all Oriental.

Murray's Inlet, Georgian Bay, July 26 1976   Onley

Murray's Inlet, Georgian Bay, July 26, 1976
'This was done looking South. I started the
painting with a fairly dry brush, then put in the
trees. I put a wash over the trees and left the
sky and the rocks the color of the paper. It's not
always what you paint but what you don't paint
that's important.'

LANDSCAPE: THE CHANGES

'Wonderfully lofty and divinely beautiful are these mountains.
In order to exhaust their marvels and grasp the work of the Creator,
one must love their spirit, study their essential features, wander
about them widely, satiate the eyes and store up the impressions in
the heart. Then, even if the eye does see the silk and one realizes
that the hand does not govern brush and ink, marvellous, mysterious,
boundless becomes that picture of mine!' KUO SSU, 11th CENTURY[15]

On an ordinary working day, Toni Onley's Silver Shadow takes him to the little airport at Boundary Bay. There he goes to the hangar and rolls his Lake Buccaneer out onto the grass. He takes time to check fuel and lubricant levels and the controls, then takes off from the soft grass runway. The airplane seems as anxious as he is to leave the flat landscape. Airborne, the plane almost silently turns toward the landscape of Toni's choice.

Flying is an important component in the artist's activity. The amphibious Lake Buccaneer, his second arplane acquired in the winter of 1974-75, allows him to go into relatively inaccessible landscape. Within minutes, he is flying over Mayne or Saturna Island, setting down at East

Point, for instance, which would otherwise be a half-day's journey by car. He can go where no roads go, much like the voyageurs of old. The landscape can be familiar, such as that of Savary Island or Harrison Lake, or almost exotic, as Vargas Island, off the West Coast of Vancouver Island. Sometimes he may go further afield. In 1975, he flew his airplane to Baffin Island in the Arctic. Every year, since 1972, he has visited and painted with Canadian sculptor and fellow pilot Robert Murray, whose summer home is on Georgian Bay. Wherever he goes, Toni Onley takes along his watercolors and paints.

The 'landings' aboard the Lake Buccaneer are somewhat different from what one may be used to in conventional airplane and seaplane travel.

On the water, the Buccaneer is a boat with its hull in the water. It can be anchored, like any other boat, or moored. Its occupants may row ashore aboard an inflatable dinghy. Or, when the presence of a hard sand or shell beach makes it possible, its landing gear allows it to be rolled ashore under power.

On cool, damp days, Onley will build a fire on the beach. This provides warmth, but it also provides a source of heat to speed up the drying of a watercolor in progress or a completed work. These can be returned to the compartment in his paint-box, and titled as to location and date later that afternoon or evening with

an osmiroid italic pen and ink.

When Toni Onley is ready to paint, no preconceived idea of what the painting will be is present in his mind; before him, Nature itself, and 'a fresh sheet, a loaded brush and infinite possibilities.'[13] He will select a form or a big shape in the landscape, often very distant, or many times magnified. This can be a headland, a rock, cloud or a combination of these. After the first shape has been transformed onto the paper, the painting's progress will be as much a result and development of it as the landscape itself. The landscape becomes a source of ideas. He will try to get some-

thing of the quality, of the mood of the landscape, but the process now takes over. The painting is both conscious and unconscious. It becomes an arrangement of landscape elements. The painting is unpredictable, much as the goat hair brush which is used to paint it. It may be very obviously a landscape, or it may become something akin to an abstraction, the result of the artist feeling his way through, responding to the watercolor more than to the landscape.

This approach is very different from the conventional idea of rendering a landscape in paint. The painter does not seek to imitate nature in a literal sense, he reacts to it, in a spirit of harmony with it, revealing through the orchestration of particular observation all nature and essential nature. This response to nature translates itself as a natural moving brush, in harmony with the spirit of the painter as he is affected by the landscape. The title may identify the location where the painting was executed, and may indeed be similar to it in configuration, but a succession of paintings done in one area, whether Saturna Island or Georgian Bay shows that there is no 'view' or representation. The landscape is there to respond to, and this response is landscape painting. This is the true depth of landscape. It is the nature of painting as such, and particularly of watercolor as a medium, that the painting is created in light.

With watercolor, the painter starts off with the total light of the sun: the white paper. It is as deep or as shallow as he wants to think about it. Spaces are created on the paper and these spaces are spaces which exist in light. It is the light on the objects that he paints, not the objects themselves, since these exist according to the condition of the day, the ambient light as affected by clouds of never ending variety and a sun which can only be in the same position in the sky once a year.

The paintings are about changes, movement. The weather conditions they suggest may be observed, or stored in the unconscious memory, to be re-created at will, according to the demands of the painting and the flowing unpredictability of the medium. Land masses are moved or removed completely. Painting has its own laws, as natural as the laws of nature. The process reveals a basic harmony with nature: a changing temperament changing with nature's constant changes. In that sense, the paintings do not fix a moment in time because they have recorded none in particular. They suggest to us all the forces at play, not only in landscape, but in painting itself. They are 'constant reminders of the beauty and mystery not of the world, but of vision'.[14] The techniques are completely subservient to the element of change and reflect it; washes and brush strokes are not totally predictable, neither is the goat hair brush. The artist has to be ready to respond in mid-stroke, to change his mind. Perhaps because they reflect these changes, the paintings of Toni Onley possess a spirit that is quite unique in Canadian landscape today.

The technique is not self-indulgent virtuosity for its own sake, but is dictated by the harmonies found in nature. These harmonies are arranged by the artist in a spirit of empathy with the landscape, its seasons and changes, life cycles and rhythms. It is English watercolor transformed by a meeting with the Orient, a meeting which is the discovery of a new world in an Ancient Nature, ever present, ever changing.

PHOTO: YUKIKO ONLEY

Toni Onley in Japan 1978

'Onley's vision of landscape reflects on the antiquity and immense endurance of the land as a reality against which the span of human existence is infinitesimal. Nature in his art is comprehended as an impersonal, neutral force, splendid in isolation rather than hostile. He does not stress the terror and sublimity of mountains as a comment on the fragility of human affairs but rather as a substantive fact that cannot be modified by the power of thought. The presence of trees is seen to be irrelevant: transitory wraiths with foliage evaporating into clouds, and trunks that are already ghosts. At any moment the land will be left once more to itself and to silently converse with the sky. The apparent solidity of things is suddenly in question; dissolution seems imminent. It is not reality that changes but art and ephemeral perceptions; the shifting view cannot indefinitely dwell on the 'Still Point'. The final impression left by these small, powerful works is of reconciliation and amazement in the presence of nature.'[15]

Dead Tree, Lookout Island, Georgian Bay, July 26 1976   Onley

Dead Tree, Lookout Island, Georgian Bay,
July 26, 1976

'The next thing I painted that day was another
dead Jack Pine. They become a beautiful gray
color which I find arresting. So I did the painting
using the dead tree as a central element, resting
it on a cross formed by the land masses in the
foreground. I love this broken symmetry. I like
the sort of awkwardness about this painting; it's a
natural quality I always hope to get in a painting.
And the grays here I find very beautiful. Strangely
enough, it has similarities with the 'White Post'
painting which I did three years earlier, but not at
the same spot.'

'Thus by living leisurely, by controlling the
vital breath, by wiping the goblet, by
playing the CH'IN, by contemplating pictures
in silence, by meditating on the four
quarters of space, by never resisting the
influence of Heaven and by responding to the call of the wilderness, where the
cliffs and peaks rise to dazzling heights
and the cloudy forests are dense and vast,
the wise and virtuous men of ancient times found innumerable
pleasures which they assimilated
by their souls and minds. What more
should I desire? If I too can find this hap-
piness in my soul; is it not better than
everything else?' TSUNG PING, FIFTH CENTURY[17]

THE PLATES

32 **Mouth of the Wanapitei River, Georgian Bay, July 30, 1976**

'I was flying with Bob Murray in his plane and noticed this river which I wanted to explore. Bob said I could explore it when we were flying in my plane. The next day, I decided to land in the smooth water; it was a very smooth landing but the plane just seemed to keep going. There is a waterfall which I would have gone over had it not been possible to veer to the right and bring the plane onto a muddy bank. Looking back towards the mouth of the river, I was interested by the rippling water running into the smooth water of the bay, and I did this painting of that contrast, based on parallel arrangements of masses.'

Mouth of the Wanapitei River, Georgian Bay, Ontario. July 30 1976

34 Beaver Pond, Lookout Island, Georgian Bay,
    August 2, 1976

'There's a beaver pond at the center of Lookout
Island. That bushy tree in the bottom helps to
establish a foreground for this broken symmetry
of an arrangement. This painting is on 'David
Cox' paper, a darker paper which I use now and
then for deeper tone. It has a richness for certain
effects which the white paper doesn't have. I
should use it more often.'

Beaver Pond Lookout Island, Georgian Bay   Aug 2 76   onley

36 Rain Cloud, Survivor's Island, Georgian Bay,
August 5, 1976
'This is a rich watercolor, color-wise. The arrangement of the pale rock shape on the right, the
darker rock in the middle … each third goes back
beyond the next shape. Antwerp Blue was used
for the water, and the sky is a mixture of Sepia
and French Ultramarine. It's almost abstract, but
you often find arrangements like that in Nature.'

Rain Cloud, Survivors Island, Georgian Bay, August 5 1976   Onley

38   Red Deer River, Alberta, August 18, 1977
        'Yukiko and I climbed over hill and dale for a week
        in the Badlands around Drumheller, Alberta,
        doing dozens of watercolors. We were exhausted
        when we arrived back at our hotel on a bend
        in the Red Deer River. The rear window of our room
        overlooked the river bend with its abstract
        arrangements of shapes, colors and contrasts. The
        painting I did turned out to be the best of
        the week.'

Red Deer River, Alberta, August 18 1977   Onley

The McCoys, Georgian Bay, July 27, 1979
'Robert Murray and I look across Georgian Bay each
summer from his Lookout Island cottage to the
McCoys, a group of pink rock islands carved by glaciers.
We wait for the wind to drop so that we can land
safely out on the open Georgian Bay in one of our flying
boats. It normally does, long enough for us to do a
few watercolors each year. I tone the pink rocks down a
bit, but Bob really does everything to make them
pink in his watercolor.'

The McCoys, Georgian Bay, July 27 1979   Onley

42   Lookout Island, Point-au-Baril, Ontario,
       July 6, 1980
       'Watercolor is not the medium for those who
       would hesitate. It offers many opportunities
       during its many stages of painting and drying,
       for example, here I dropped water into an
       almost dry sky. This picked up the pigment and
       carried it to the edge, creating a cloud. Just
       as nature conforms to its own rules, one must
       understand the nature of one's painting
       medium and work within it.'

Lookout Island, Point au Baril, Ontario, July 6 1980   Owley

44   Lookout Island, Georgian Bay, July 6, 1980
'There is a very strange rock formation on the
south side of the Island, like a whale coming out
of the water, and the rock is broken clean into
three parts, like a fallen column by water freezing
and expanding. The trees on the horizon were
done with a partially dry brush, and I painted over
the whole foreground with one color – Lamp
Black and Winsor Blue combined, in order to send
the eye into the middle and far distance.'

Lookout Island, Georgian Bay, July 6 1980   Bentley

46   Green Water, Murray's Inlet, Lookout Island,
      Point-au-Baril, Georgian Bay, July 9, 1980
      'I did this after supper because it had been a hot
      day and I hadn't been able to do much. The trees were
      really dark because the sun was setting behind
      them, but the mosquitoes were so ferocious that I had
      to paint it very quickly. That's probably why it's
      the best thing I did that day.'

Green water, Murray's Inlet, Lookout Island, Point au Baril, Georgian Bay, July 9 1980   Onley

48   Ghost Tree, Lookout Island, Georgian Bay,
      Ontario, July 10, 1980
      'I had painted this tree in there but I really didn't
      like it, so I painted it out. What was left of it I really
      liked. Like a disappearing shape, so I thought I'd
      even bring more attention to it with a composition
      based on a cross arrangement. The symmetry's
      a bit off to make it more interesting.'

ghost Tree, Lookout Island, georgian Bay, Ontario, July 10 1980   onley

50   Lookout Island, Point-au-Baril, Ontario,
     July 12, 1980
     'The rocks at Georgian Bay are smooth and
     round because of the glacial action of the ice age.
     Those clouds were really a group of trees
     which looked too ordinary, so I washed them out.
     I guess I really like doing that.'

Lookout Island, Point Aubois, Ontario, July 12 1980   Owley

52 East Point, Saturna Island, B.C.,
    August 5, 1980
    'Just below the old lighthouse near East Point, there's
    a beautiful little beach which I can run the plane
    up on. I painted two logs there of different colors. They
    suggested clouds to me, so I painted clouds above.
    That looked ordinary too, so I painted a shadow under
    the cloud, adding an element of ambiguity. I liked
    the result and I even derived a print from it which I think
    was really successful, the proof being that no one's
    bought it.'

East Point, Saturna Island, B.C. August 5 1980   Oxley

54 Black Mountain, B.C., August 16, 1980
'This is what I saw from Shingle Point in Trincomali
Channel. It's actually the point of an island, but
I didn't put the peninsula in, I just wanted that great
triangle. It's another of my almost symmetrical
arrangements. Really strong too.'

Black Mountain, B.C. August 16 1980
owley

56   Haro Strait from Saturna Island, B.C.,
     September 12, 1980
     'I was at East Point again, looking towards Orcas
     Island in Washington. The top of the island was
     disappearing into an afternoon build-up of clouds.
     I did a print based on this one called Georgian
     Strait. Like the islands disappearing into the
     clouds, it's hard to know where Haro Strait ends
     and Georgian Strait begins.'

Haro Strait from Saturna Island, B.C. September 12 1980   Onley

58 Forest Fire, Vancouver Island,
October 2, 1980
'This is really the pulp mill at Chemainus on
Vancouver Island painted from Tent Island. I really
got so absorbed in this one that I didn't notice
that I'd put my thumb-print on it when I picked
the painting up and put it against a rock to look at.
But it doesn't detract from the work. This is
probably one of the first times I've ever painted
smoke, and I quite like it. Smoke rises on a
calm day until it reaches upper levels where there
is wind, then it all goes off to one direction.'

Forest Fire, Vancouver Island, October 2 1980

60 Restless Sea, October 16, 1980
'I know it's a cliché to paint waves, but I can't help it,
I find it very challenging. They change constantly and
they move very quickly. You just have to look at
them again and again and try to memorize what it's
doing, then you paint it and don't look back. This
is one of the better wave paintings I've done. I could
paint waves forever and be quite satisfied because
they're almost impossible to paint, that's why I have to
try. The water here is Winsor Green and black, and
I added Winsor Blue to part of it. Under the wave it's
Sepia and Winsor Green, and there's Antwerp
Blue on the horizon, which is partially wiped to make
it disappear into the sky.'

Restless sea,   october 16 1980   owley

62 Fog, Winter Cove, Saturna Island, B.C.,
    October 21, 1980
    'It was a misty day with the fog rolling in at the
    top of the trees. I was a bit worried that I wouldn't
    be able to fly out again. I did those trees with one
    brush stroke with pigment in the tip of the brush
    and water in the butt. I made an oil painting based
    on this one …'

fog. winter cove, saturna island, B.C. october 21 1980   onley

64   Ridge Cloud, Saturna Island, B.C.,
        October 26, 1980
        'Clouds are infinitely variable because they are
        constantly changing. They dissolve and
        remake themselves almost like the seabreeze
        climbs a hillside and condenses time
        upon time, creating new shapes and lights
        for me to see and perhaps to paint.
        It's as if the meeting of moisture and land
        created them. This is the process that
        creates the patterns for me to choose from
        and paint.'

Ridge cloud, Saturna Island, B.C., October 26 1980   onley

66   Saturna Island, B.C., February 6, 1981
'The water that surrounds the islands of this
coast somehow situates them in space, and you
often see land masses as receding planes in
space. When light gets mixed up with this, you
can have an infinite number of possibilities.
Here, light appearing behind the dark peninsula
is white before the lighter gray land mass, but
there's another darker one behind that because
it has less light. But clouds themselves are
masses in front and behind each other, in various
densities. There's no reason why you can't
treat clouds as you do rocks in a painting, because
the light can make rocks as soft as clouds,
and softer.'

Saturna Island, B.C. February 6 1981   Onley

68   White Island, B.C., February 6, 1981
'The Island in the middle distance is lighter
than the sky in this, perhaps the loosest painting
in the book. I painted it very quickly, and when
I saw how well defined an edge appeared in the
foreground painted in rich and deep sand
colors. I thought the sky could be like a ghostly
repetition, almost an after-image or reflection
of the land in the water of the cloud.'

White Island, B.C. February 6 1981   Onley

70 Three Rocks, Savage Point, B.C.,
February 8, 1981
'There seems to be lots of unpleasantness
associated with Savage Point, as its name would
suggest. There are reefs, dangerous tides and
it is exposed to the prevailing weather. The three
rocks on this point of Tumbo Island provide
a good contrast to the clouds which seém to rise
from the water, as if the vapors are condensing.
Water is becoming clouds, in this very wet
watercolor.'

Three Rocks, Savage point, B.C. February 8 1981   owley

72   **Reefs, Boundary Pass, B.C., February 22, 1981**
'This very atmospheric watercolor is based on
what I saw looking south across the water to the
mountains of the Olympic peninsula, dark and
light snow-capped mountains. Two dark, pointed
reefs cross each other, echoing the mountains
that rise and almost merge with it.'

Reefs, Boundary Pass, B.C. Feb 22 1981   Onley

74 **Mainland Mountains from Tumbo Island, B.C., February 22, 1981**

'From this little island, you can see the Cascade mountains to the east of Mount Baker. But when you do, they are quite often on a single plane, which may or may not work in a painting. In this instance, I lifted all the color in the middle of the mountains with one big sweep of the brush, to bring them to life, the perfect answer to the dark beach foreground.'

Mainland Mountains from Tumbo Is. B.C. Feb 22 1981   Onley

76 Tumbo Channel, B.C., February 28, 1981

'When I go to Tumbo Island, I usually land in a
little bay on the south side of the island, but
this time, the wind was wrong, and I had to land
in Tumbo Channel. I taxied towards a group
of rocks and found a smooth rocky shelf there
where I could beach the plane. It was a great
spot, full of raw beauty. I did six paintings that day.
There were great views. This one is derived
from three bands of rocks, over which I put in
three trees, hardly distinguishable except
for their trunks. Saturna Island appears in the
distance. My trees are forever evaporating
into the distance, it seems. I don't get involved
with them as trees, just as compositional
elements. In this painting, the most solid shape
is the water, while the landscape flows like
water. The color of that water is the result of
mixing Winsor Blue and black.'

Tumbo Channel, B.C. February 28 1981   Crowley

78   Mt. Cheam over Harrison Lake, B.C.,
February 29, 1981

'March 1st is the actual date, according to my
flight log, when I flew into Harrison Lake. I don't
know how many times I've painted Mount
Cheam over Harrison Lake. It's one of the places
I keep going back to. I land about half way up
Harrison Lake and put the plane down on one of
the many little coves and beaches on the west
side of the lake, for a good view of Mount Cheam.
Many times, my paintings here are a bit too
descriptive of the landscape and not as involved
with painting as I would like. Treated loosely
and abstractly, the landscape here is fragile. This
is one of those paintings that just seemed to
paint itself. I watched it come together before me.
It's like being possessed. You almost feel guilty
when that happens. Or blessed.'

Mt. Cheam over Harrison Lake, B.C. February 27 1981   onley

80 White Island, Boundary Pass, B.C.,
March 4, 1981
'Sometimes, the forms which are clouds, islands
and water are elusive and all come together.
Clouds drain themselves into water, or water is
siphoned up into clouds, dissolving land
masses. It's like all the elements of nature inter-
mingling, mixing with one another. Nothing
is separate from anything else, and watercolor
says this better than any other medium.'

White Island, Boundary Pass. B.C. March 4 1961   Onley

Green Island, Narvaez Bay, Saturna Island,
B.C., March 4, 1981

'That day, I landed in a rugged little bay on the
South side of Saturna Island. I rarely land
there because the sea is usually too rough. That
side of the Island is rather precipitous and
everything there seems to be bigger than life.
There are big storms, big trees, big rocks
with interesting formations. It's not a very gentle
part of the Island. In fact the landscape is
a bit frightening, that's why the wildlife is abun-
dant there. I was able to taxi onto the beach.
This watercolor shows water which seems partly
solid and partly soluble, and landscape
which is partly solid but can be dissolved by
low clouds.'

green Island, Narvaez Bay, Saturna Island, B.C. March 4 1981   Onley

84 Narvaez Bay, Saturna Island, B.C.,
March 4, 1981

'On one side of the bay there is a group of
rocks which present an endless variety of shapes
and shadows to paint. They are fallen pieces
of the island. I must have done a dozen paintings of
these rocks, of which this is one. As I painted
there, an old recluse came out of the woods towards
me. His clothes were in tatters, held together
by safety pins. There were holes in his shoes and
he hadn't shaved in months or years. Very
abruptly he asked: "Having trouble, young fellow?",
unaccustomed to the visit of a plane on the
beach. "No, no trouble," I said, "just came in here
to do a painting." "Fine," he said. It could
almost have been an everyday occurrence for him.'

Navarez Bay, Saturna Island, B.C. March 4 1981 ———— Onley

Narvaez Bay, Saturna Island, B.C
March 8, 1981

'This painting reminds me of the big abstract
paintings I was doing in the early Sixties, where
shapes were placed in such a way as to point
to the painting's edges, describing the format or
the space. I guess I still like doing that. I pur-
posely made the horizon a bit crooked here so
that it could also be the underside of a cloud.
I like to make people question what they see. I
think they should, because when we're
painting, we're also describing what we're not
painting, and that's when painting gets
exciting. This one is painted around that void,
which is almost the most concrete shape
in the painting.'

Misty Bay, Saturna Island, B.C. March 8 1981   Bouley

88   Black Island, Haro Strait, B.C., March 8, 1981

'I started by painting the shapes of some big logs which were washed up on the shore, and I painted some of them over, but I left some white paper as a highlight on a log and also as bright light on the water's horizon. Those logs direct your eye out of the painting, but the island at left of center brings you back.'

Black Island, Haro Strait, B.C. March 8 1981   onley

Island, Narvaez Bay, Saturna Island, B.C.,
March 8, 1981

'I had been painting for over an hour, and the
hermit came out of the woods again towards
me. "Have you finished your painting?", he asked.
It was as if I had last seen him an hour earlier,
rather than four days and a dozen paintings ago.
This time, I was absorbed in a black rock
which formed a little island in the bay. The water
has eroded it, creating interesting patterns of
light and shadow.'

Island, Narvaez Bay, Saturna Island, B.C. March 8 1981   onley

92 Headland, Montague Bay, Galiano Island, B.C.,
March 9, 1981

'This is sort of an enigma. I had painted the foreground
and a land mass in the middle distance, and it was
uninteresting. That's what happens quite often when you
are more aware of the landscape than you are about
the painting. The painting brings you back to reality. So this
time, I turned my back to the landscape and decided
to repaint the headland, bringing it in closer to the foreground, and ending at a partial reflection of itself, as
if unresolved. A successful painting should be 'unresolved'
so that the viewer can complete it himself. Paintings
which are finished in a predictable way are not as succcessful.
It's the paintings that are finished in an unpredictable
way that are the paintings that you live for.'

Headland, Montague Bay, Galiano Island, B.C. August 9 1981   Onley

94 Drift Logs, Montague Bay, Galiano Island,
B.C., March 9, 1981
'After all the tension of the previous painting, I
was determined to make the next one loose.
I played with the shapes of the logs evaporating
into water and turning into sky, always trying
to keep it as simple as possible. Fortunately, this
was another painting that was effortless.'

Drift logs. Montague Bay, Galiano Island, B.C. March 4 1981   Onley

96   **Montague Bay, Galiano Island, B.C., March 9, 1981**
'Looking north, I noticed that rocks near the shore
were like fingers extended or even tree roots.
They provided a good contrast to the headland in
the background which partially dissolves into
the sky. All the diagonal lines of the painting are
fixed by the two dark rock shapes to the left,
which could also be trees.'

Montague Bay, Galiano Island, B.C. March 9 81   onley

98   James Island, B.C., March 9, 1981

'I've never set foot on this island, but I've painted
it over and over again. Its dark form seems to rise out
of the waters of Trincomali Channel. I applied bold
brush strokes to the foreground, but these 'logs' were
washed ashore from the painting more than from
the landscape itself, echoing the layers of cloud over
the horizon, before and behind the island.'

James Island, B.C. March 9 1981

100   White Cloud, James Island, B.C., March 9, 1981

'While doing the last painting, I noticed that some
of the elements in it were centered, so in
this painting I decided to emphasize the three
stacked shapes of cloud, mountain and log.
To offset the obvious symmetry, I left half of the
foreground white and was pleased with the
result. This was the most abstract painting of
that day's work.'

white cloud, James Island, B.C. March 9 1981 onley

102 Pitt Lake, B.C., March 10, 1981

'There are ten paintings in this book of Pitt Lake.
As I have often done before, I flew there on
March 10 and again on March 11. Pitt Lake is an
ever-changing landscape: the weather makes
it so. The changes can be so sudden that the water
will be calm in one area and rippled in another.
On both days, I landed the plane at a small point
on the western shore where Defrauder Creek
tumbles into the lake in a great waterfall. There is
a little hermit cabin there; its occupant was
either absent or oblivious to my coming and going.
From this point, you can see a procession of
dark mountains to the east, some of them snow-
capped. The weather often seems to come
up from behind.'

Pitt Lake, B.C. March 16 1981   Onley

104 Osprey Mountain, Pitt Lake, B.C., March 10, 1981

'The lakes to the north of the Fraser River are all very
different from one another. They all drain their
glacial waters into the Fraser, but in fact they appear
to be large reservoirs of water left from some
ancient flood, trapped by mountains. Pitt Lake seems
narrower than the other lakes and is slightly
ominous. There is something foreboding about it. The
place seems to be possessed by a spirit and you
almost feel that spirit will reach out and snatch you from
the sky. If there are monsters in some lakes, there
is sure to be one in Pitt Lake. I'm always extra-careful
when I fly there and double-check all the
equipment.'

Osprey Mountain, Pitt Lake, B.C. March 10 1981   Mowley

106   Three Mountains, Pitt Lake, B.C.,
March 10, 1981

'If the lake has its demons, there is a spirit in the skies. Clouds appear and disappear, and the three mountains are constantly changing forms, according to light and weather. They stand between the water above and the water below. They are solid and massive, yet one feels that their forms could be completely evaporated by the waters.'

Three Mountains, Pitt Lake, B.C. March 10 1981   Onley

108   Pitt Lake, B.C., March 10, 1981
        'I can't remember having gone to Pitt Lake without
        it raining. It doesn't really interrupt me when
        the rain is brief and intermittent or falling elsewhere.
        This very wet painting will suggest the wetness
        of the place. The rainswept sky can veil the mountains
        and the horizon may or may not contrast sharply
        with their forms.'

Pitt lake, B.C. March 10 1981   Onley

110   Goose Island, Pitt Lake, March 11, 1981
'I went back to the same spot the next day, and
the weather was different. It was a good day and
towards evening when I flew back home I had
six paintings. This one is based on the view of The
Golden Ears (Mount Blanshard), with Goose
Island in the middle-ground, almost at its foot. A
shaft of sunlight on the water made it shine
brighter than the water near me.'

goose Island, Pitt Lake, B.C. March 11, 1981   onley

112 Coast Mountains, Pitt Lake, B.C.,
March 11, 1981
'An interesting mountain towards the north and
across the lake has many interesting shapes
which I used for a portion of this painting. Then
I used a headland further south for more
interest and a better arrangement. Its ghostly
reflection adds interest to the water, while
beyond the headland, light and mist create
their own forms.'

Coast Mountains, Pitt Lake, B.C. March 11 1981   Onley

114   Mt. Osprey and Mt. Blanshard over Pitt Lake, B.C.,
March 11, 1981

'In this painting, I wanted the two lighter snow-capped
peaks on one plane, so I compressed the landscape
a bit and changed the shape of the darker mountain. Then,
I brought out the snow-capped peaks by painting the
dark clouds behind them. The water was a monochrome
greyish green, so I added interest to the foreground
by dragging a dryer brush nearer the shore.'

Mt. Osprey and Mt. Blanchard over Pitt Lake, B.C. March 11 1981   Onley

116 **Little Goose Island, Pitt Lake, B.C., March 11, 1981**
'Headlands dissolve into each other while clouds
and mists disperse to reveal the light on the
mountain. Its white shape is echoed by the dark
form of the island. The foreground consists
of wide brushstrokes. The composition is simple,
but effective.'

Little goose Island, Pitt Lake, B.C. March 11 1981   owley

118 Golden Ears over Pitt Lake, B.C.,
March 11, 1981
'I like this one best of all. It is painted with
various mixtures of Alizarin Crimson and Winsor
Green. The sharp edges of the dark and lighter
mountains contrast with the vaporous skies and
the water. The horizon is indefinite, as if a mist
hovers on and over the lake.'

golden Firs, over pitt lake, B.C. March 11 1981   onley

120   **Mt. Higgins over Pitt Lake, March 11, 1981**
'Because the afternoon light obscures almost
everything at lower altitudes, the meeting point of
water and mountain is indefinite; the water is
quiet, as if sleeping. The sky is still active; light and
clouds create patterns. The mountain is
more clearly defined in the low late light of the
afternoon.'

Mr. Higgins over Pitt Lake, B.C. March 11 1981   Onley

122   Mt. Robie Reid, Stave Lake, B.C.,
        March 12, 1981
        'On March 12, I flew to Stave Lake, to the east of
        Pitt Lake. Before landing, I flew over the glacier
        on Mount Robie Reid and fixed its pattern in my
        memory. I landed at Glacier Point towards the
        north end of the lake. The first thing I did was to
        paint what I remembered seeing, because you
        can't get a clear view of the mountain from that
        point.'

Mt. Robbie Reid, Pitt Lake, B.C. March 12, 1981   Bowler

124   **Mt. Breier over Stave Lake, B.C., March 12, 1981**
        'Looking north, one could see Mt. Breier under the
        clouds. The headland on the left is probably
        Cottage Point. Its heavy mass was a good foil for the
        old twisted logs on the rock shelf in the fore-
        ground. The water of the lake was almost a large
        flat shape, so I painted it like that.'

Mt. Freier over Stave Lake, B.C. March 12, 1981   Doley

126   Mt. Benvolio and Diavolo Glacier, Garibaldi
Park, B.C., March 12, 1981
'When I was putting the Mt. Breier watercolor
away in my paint box, I saw the Mt. Robie Reid watercolor upside down. It suggested another
arrangement, so I developed that idea, working
around the mountain forms quite freely.
The result was very interesting; the composition
seems to take place on opposite sides
of a diagonal line, repeated, and opposed by two
diagonal lines in the opposite direction
that don't quite meet the first.'

Mt. Benvolio and Diavolo glacier, garibaldi Park, B.C. March 12 1981 Onley

128   Glacier Bay, Stave Lake, B.C., March 12, 1981
'This further interpretation of Mt. Robie Reid is
more insistent on the mountain's structure, a bit
emphasized here. The sky is like a wind current
going up the mountain. The lake is treated freely,
as a distraction from the strong pattern of the
mountain's triple peaks.'

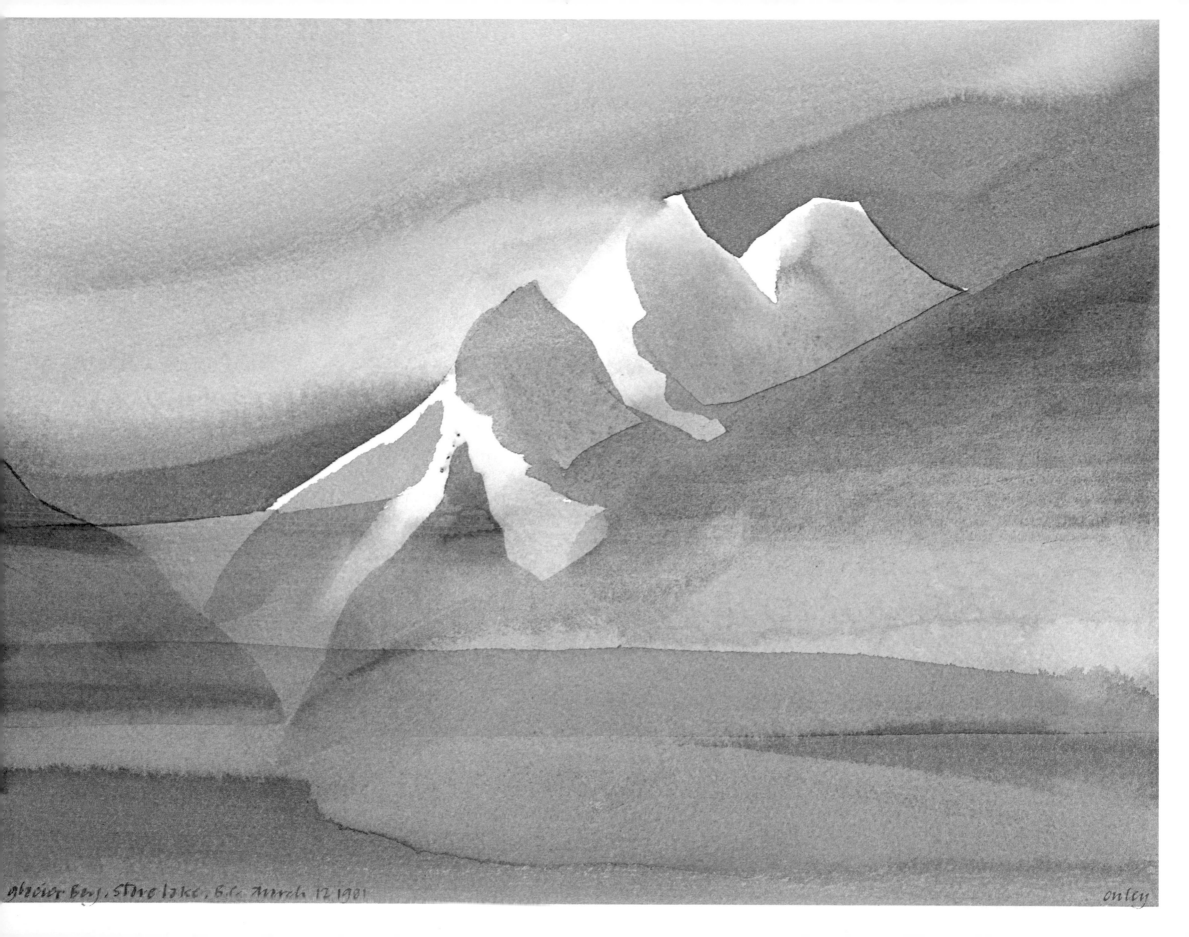

Glacier Bays, Stone lake, B.C. March 12 1901   Onley

130   **Mt. Baker from Tumbo Island, B.C.,**
            March 20, 1981

            'Many painters have turned their backs
on the mountains because they are too pretty.
They declare them unpaintable. But they
are different to me. They provide me with upright
forms beyond their natural beauty. Mt. Baker
has a most satisfying shape, assymetrical, with a
rounded top. The contour of the volcano is
almost a calligraphic line. The mountain rises
above the water, as if born from it. How
could I not paint it?'

Mt. Baker from Tumbo Island, B.C. March 20,1981   enley

132   Oak Trees, Tumbo Island, B.C.,
      March 20, 1981
      'My now familiar dissolving trees: I like to think that
      everything in nature is part of everything else.
      The trees are interesting. They interrupt the flow of
      the landscape from one side to the other as
      does the crescent of beach. The sky is almost solid.'

Oak Trees, Tumbo Island, B.C. March 20 1981   Onley

134 **Cascade Mountains across the Strait of Georgia, B.C., March 20, 1981**

'Looking east from Tumbo Island, one can often see the Cascade mountain range from Washington state. The rise seems to begin at the water, and goes to the clouds that often form at the summits. Variable winds cause the water to appear in different colors, as does a cloudy sky. Panoramic landscapes such as this are plentiful in this area, and this is one of the best.'

Cascade Mountains, across the strait of Georgia, B.C., March 20 1981   Onley

136   St. John Point, Mayne Island, B.C.,
April 7, 1981
'I landed my plane in Winter Cove that day, a
day with marvelous clouds. The moist air current
rising becomes a cloud at a certain altitude,
meeting other clouds at different levels. This
painting is based on a very strong cross
arrangement. I was very pleased with this one
and in May, I made an oil painting of the
same subject.'

St John point, Mayne Island, B.C., April 7 1981   oulcy

138   Storm Cloud, Strait of Georgia, B.C.,
April 7, 1981

'Two horizontal bands of water, near and far …
This is a cloud painting pure and simple, but rich
and active. The painting is even more "real" as a
result of those spots at the upper left corner
formed by falling rain drops.'

Storm Cloud, Strait of Georgia, B.C. April 7 1981   Onley

140   Strait of Georgia, B.C., April 7, 1981

'The three rocks or islands in the stretches of
water bring you to a valley in the clouds
which could almost be a valley between two
mountains. The sky was always dramatic
that day and paintings happened as naturally
as the sky changed.'

Strait of Georgia, B.C. from Samuel Island, April 7 1981 · onley

142   Gulf Island, B.C., April 7, 1981
       'The fourth painting that day was a mountain and
       sky picture. The mountain-island and water
       are almost one as the light seems to come from
       the back. This light permeates all the clouds.
       Raindrops fell on the painting again, warning me
       I had better leave for home. So I did, quite
       pleased with the day's painting.'

gulf Islands, B.C. April 7 1981   onley

144   Footnotes

1. Donald Buchanon, "The Paintings and Drawings of F. H. Varley," Canadian Art, VII, No. 1, (1949) 3.

2. Alexander Cozens, "A New Method of Landscape" (1975) Reprinted by the Paddington Press Ltd., (1977), p.2.

3. Idem, p.8-9.

4. Osvald Siren, "The Chinese on the Art of Painting," (New York: Schocken Books) 1963, p.106. (Originally published in 1936)

5. Idem, p.107.

6. Toni Onley, "Japan Diary," Vancouver: The Vancouver Art Gallery (Vanguard) September 1978, p.5.

7. Alexander Cozens, "A New Method of Landscape" (1785) Reprinted by the Paddington Press Ltd. (1977) p.23.

8. Idem, p.8.

9. Osvald Siren, "The Chinese on the Art of Painting," (New York: Schocken Books) 1963, p.24. (Originally published in 1936).

10. Toni Onley, "Japan Diary," Vancouver: The Vancouver Art Gallery (Vanguard) September 1978, p.5.

11. Osvald Siren, "The Chinese on the Art of Painting," (New York: Schocken Books) 1963, p.79-80.

12. Idem, p.82.

13. Toni Onley, "Japan Diary," Vancouver: The Vancouver Art Gallery (Vanguard) September 1978, p.5.

14. Ted Lindberg, "Toni Onley, A Retrospective Exhibition" (Vancouver, The Vancouver Art Gallery), 1978.

15. Michael Greenwood, "The Canadian Canvas" (Toronto: Arts Canada) March 1975, p.15.

16. Osvald Siren, "The Chinese on the Art of Painting," (New York: Schocken Books) 1963, p.48.

17. Idem, p.16.